Pebble® Plus

Dance, Dance, Dance

Ballet Dancing

by Kathryn Clay

Consulting editor: Gail Saunders-Smith, PhD

Content consultant: Heidi L. Schimpf,
Director of Programs and Services
Joy of Motion Dance Center
Washington, D.C.

CAPSTONE PRESS
a capstone imprint

Pebble Plus is published by Capstone Press,
151 Good Counsel Drive, P.O. Box 669, Mankato, Minnesota 56002.
www.capstonepress.com

092009
005618CGS10

 Books published by Capstone Press are manufactured with paper
containing at least 10 percent post-consumer waste.

Library of Congress Cataloging-in-Publication Data
Clay, Kathryn.
    Ballet dancing / by Kathryn Clay.
    p. cm. — (Pebble plus. Dance, dance, dance)
    Includes bibliographical references and index.
    Summary: "Simple text and photographs present ballet dancing,
including simple steps" — Provided by publisher.
    ISBN 978-1-4296-4002-2 (library binding)
    1. Ballet — Juvenile literature. I. Title. II. Series.
GV1787.5.C53 2010
792.8 — dc22   2009023378

Editorial Credits
Jennifer Besel, editor; Veronica Bianchini, designer;
    Marcie Spence, media researcher; Eric Manske, production specialist

Photo Credits
All photos by Capstone Studio/Karon Dubke

The Capstone Press Photo Studio thanks Dance Express in
Mankato, Minnesota, and The Dance Connection in Rosemount,
Minnesota, for their help with photo shoots for this book.

Note to Parents and Teachers

The Dance, Dance, Dance series supports national physical education standards and the
national standards for learning and teaching dance in the arts. This book describes and
illustrates ballet. The images support early readers in understanding the text. The repetition of
words and phrases helps early readers learn new words. This book also introduces early readers
to subject-specific vocabulary words, which are defined in the Glossary section. Early readers
may need assistance to read some words and to use the Table of Contents, Glossary, Read
More, Internet Sites, and Index sections of the book.

Table of Contents

All about Ballet

Point your toes,

and turn in a circle.

It's fun to dance ballet

with friends.

Ballet uses movement

to tell a story.

Dancers need strong muscles

to move smoothly.

What to Wear

Ballet dancers

wear soft slippers.

Slippers bend easily

to help dancers

point their toes.

Dancers wear leotards

and tights

when they practice.

They practice in studios.

Dancers wear costumes
or tutus for recitals.
They perform recitals
on big stages.

Sweet Steps

Ballet has five positions.

Dancers learn

where to hold

their arms and legs.

First

Second

Third

Fourth

Fifth

Ballet dancers bend their knees.

This move is called a plié.

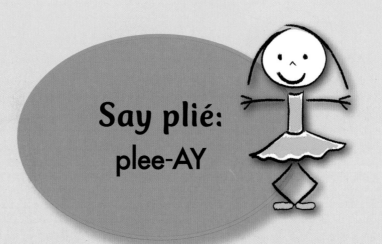

Say plié:
plee-AY

Dancers balance on one foot.

Then they turn.

This move is called a pirouette.

Say pirouette: peer-ah-WET

Ready to Dance

Bend, turn, and jump

to the music.

Take a bow!

Glossary

balance — to keep steady and not fall

leotard — a tight piece of clothing worn by dancers

muscle — a body part that pulls on bones to make them move

position — the way a dancer stands; ballet has five positions.

recital — a show where people dance for others

studio — a room or building where a dancer practices

tutu — a short ballet skirt made of several layers of stiff net

Read More

Castle, Kate. *My First Ballet Book.* Boston: Kingfisher, 2006.

Hackett, Jane. *Ballerina: A Step-by-Step Guide to Ballet.* New York: DK, 2007.

Nelson, Marilyn. *Beautiful Ballerina.* New York: Scholastic Press, 2009.

Internet Sites

FactHound offers a safe, fun way to find Internet sites related to this book. All of the sites on FactHound have been researched by our staff.

Here's all you do:

Visit *www.facthound.com*

FactHound will fetch the best sites for you!

Index

Word count: 116
Grade: 1
Early-Intervention Level: 14